I0004746

ONLINE

Written By

JANET GREENWALD
&
LAURA GREENWALD

**Published by Get Your Stuff Together Productions
For Lion And The Rock Entertainment**

LION AND THE ROCK
ENTERTAINMENT

Copyright © 2016, 2020 The Next of Kin Education Project
All rights reserved, including the right to reproduce this book or portions thereof in any form whatsoever.

"My Social Life", "Get Your Stuff Together," "Ready In 10" and the forms and plans within, should be used for general information purposes only. Readers using the information herein, agree to hold NOKEP, Ready In 10 Network, Stuf Productions and the authors, harmless from any liability incurred by its use. All information contained within is copyrighted and may not be republished without written permission.

For information about special discounts and bulk purchases go to www.getyourstufftogether.com
or email us at corpsales@getyourstufftogether.com

Manufactured in the United States of America

ISBN: 978-1536814323

Table Of Contents

Before You Begin   2

My Social Life Forms   4

    Social Media Accounts & Blogs   6

    Voice Mail Accounts   10

    Personal Email Accounts   11

    Internet Memberships   12

My Business Life Forms   20

    My Business Email Addresses   22

    Business Websites   23

    Pay Pal or Shopping Cart Management Accounts   25

    Contractors/Virtual Assistants   25

    Affiliate Accounts   26

    Publishing Accounts   27

    Email List Management Accounts   28

    Business Bank Accounts   28

    Our Business Structure   29

    Business Credit Cards   30

    Office Rental Information   30

    Business Insurance   31

Memberships/ID Cards   31

My Business' Social Media   32

Internet Memberships   39

Other Websites That I Often Use   41

Office Inventory   43

My Social Media Will   45

FOREWORD

I met Laura and Janet Greenwald nearly a decade ago as our paths crossed in the Next of Kin/ Emergency Contact field. Their efforts included new legislation with U.S. Representative Jesse Jackson, Jr. and a highly successfully national campaign to educate hospitals and Americans on the importance of Next of Kin Notification. Their passion and steam was sadly born out of personal loss and frustration with the system. But this dynamic team has taken this personal tragedy and expanded on it to help and educate all of us.

In America like many other countries, we battle the complacency factor, living as if we will never need to prepare for emergencies. I've seen my share of overnight visionaries, many born out of the various global and daily disasters I deal with. These efforts though commendable sadly lose the momentum and fail to last or impress me or the world we live in. I've truly only met one team who has battled through and will change the way we get prepared, and that is the Greenwalds.

This book will profoundly change the way you protect yourself and your family. Life does not give many second chances or a rewind button, so trust in the expertise of Janet and Laura Greenwald.

Mark V. Cerney
President/Founder Next of Kin Registry (NOKR)

Before You Begin

Before You Begin

This book is a little different than most books, because it comes with all of the forms that you need to keep your social media account information at your fingertips, in a digital format. Just go to www.getyourstufftogether.com/castcrew/onlinedigdwld.zip to download the forms, fill them in and save them to your computer, a flash drive, portable hard drive, smartphone and yes even The Cloud.

This way if you need a copy of your social media logons quickly, you can retrieve them from any Internet-enabled computer, cellphone or tablet, enabling you to deal with emergencies large and small, even when you're away from home.

You'll also notice that there are two parts to the book. The first section is for your personal logins, passwords and URLs and the second, for your business. If you need more space, just add lines to the downloadable documents or print out the forms and put them into a notebook. Once you've completed the My Social Life forms and Social Media Will, we suggest that you save and store them in at least three secure locations, preferably away from home – just in case.

Besides the copy that you'll save to your iCloud or Dropbox account, save your files **on a password-protected flash drive or portable hard drive:**

- And take it with you during evacuation on a key ring or in your evacuation bin.
- And place it in a safe deposit box or water/fireproof safe in your own city.
- And place it in a safe deposit box, water/fireproof safe, or with relatives in the city where you'll be evacuating.
- Or place the forms and documents in a password-protected online file repository or the file directory of your family's personal web site.

You can also simply fill in the forms right in the book, along with your Social Media Will and toss it into your file cabinet, safe deposit box, glove compartment, emergency bin, or had it to your lawyer. It's up to you.

Online is based on our book *Keep Everything Your Love Safe*. As we always say, the best way to avoid loss is to prevent it. By completing the Forms in this book, you'll be well on your way to keeping preventable loss away from yourself and the people that you love. And when you're ready to take your preparations a step further, be sure to check out *Ready* on the book tab of www.getyourstufftogether.com.

My Social Life Forms

Your Web & Social Media Forms

If you're like most people, you know your Email, Facebook, Social Media and Voicemail Usernames & Passwords by heart – or at least your computer does. But what if you have to use someone else's phone or computer, or only have a few seconds to reach your family or update your friends in an emergency?

Would you remember ALL that information off the top of your head?

Probably not.

And we're not just talking about emergencies. Imagine not having to remember which account it was that made you add two numbers and three symbols to your password before they would let you sign up. It's probably the one you only have to log in to once every six months.

Of course that's exactly why you let your computer memorize the logons for you in the first place. Which is fine until the computer decides to upgrade your Internet browser and clear your password cache without your permission, or your computer crashes and takes your logon information along with it.

It makes a lot more sense to have them all written down in one place – along with any instructions you or someone else using them on your behalf, might need.

So if you're ready, let's give all those user IDs, passwords and logins a place to live.

Your mission is to create a list of all your social media, email, internet and voice mail account passwords, usernames and other important information, not only for you to refer to, but in case you or your family needs that info ASAP.

And The Password Is…

Grab a pencil and paper and, on the downloadable forms that came with this book or the forms in the back of the book, jot down the types of Social Media, Email, Voice Mail and any Internet Based Accounts and Favorite Web Sites that you must log into to use.

Here are a few ideas to get you started:
- Facebook, Twitter, Google Plus, LinkedIn, YouTube, Pinterest, Flickr, Instagram
- Your Personal and Work Email Accounts
- Your Home, Cell Phone and Work Voicemail
- Your iTunes, Pandora, Blogs, Cloud/File Storage Sites, Kindle Accounts

- Internet-based Memberships With Recurring Fees like Netflix, Hulu, News Sites, or Professional Organizations.

Getting Them Down On Paper

Using the list you just compiled, locate and write down the usernames, passwords and any other information you need to log in for each account on the list.

Depending on where you have them saved right now, this will take anywhere from:

- Five Seconds (you already have a list to refer to)
- To Several Hours (you have to go to each and every site to find that information)

Here's What Goes In The Sheet

The Social Media Information Sheet is broken into separate sections for each type of account. For each account you have, fill in your username, password, the URL you use to log in, the email address you used to register the account and what you use it for. For example, you might have one Facebook account for your personal use and one for your business.

For voice mail accounts be sure to list dial in numbers, passwords, what it's for (cell, work, landline) and any instructions, notes, tips for using it or updating it.

For paid web memberships, note the fee, when and how it's paid, your customer number and any customer service numbers or contacts.

Running Out Of Space?

If you're using our digital Social Media Info Sheet and need to add more space or entries for accounts that aren't on the original sheet, simply add additional pages to the Word document, then cut and paste the information from part of the document into the new page. Then edit it to add the information you need. Just remember to save it with a different name so you don't overwrite the original file.

Work Benefits Information

On the Social Media Sheets, you'll also find a section for your Work Benefits Information & Passwords. If you work for a large company or a non-profit you probably get quite a few benefits that you only use a few times a year (and never remember how to log in!).

For instance, the employee website with your health insurance elections, life insurance or 401K preferences or employee discounts and associate rewards.

Be sure to note all of your User IDs/Passwords, HR or Benefits Representatives, Customer Service Numbers, Member IDs and any special instructions that would help your spouse or family access the information or activate a benefit in an emergency.

Where To Store The List For Safekeeping

Where and how you store copies of the information sheet is up to you. Here are a few ideas to get you started.

- Store a copy on a password protected file on your computer hard drive.
- Store a copy on a password protected flash or portable hard drive and place it in your local safe deposit box.
- Store a copy on a password protected flash or portable hard drive and place it in your a safe deposit box in your pre-determined evacuation location.
- Store a copy on a password-protected online file repository or on the file directory of your family's personal web site. This way, you can retrieve them from any Internet-enabled computer.
- You can also store a copy along with your will or important papers at your attorney's office.

And While You're At It…

Be sure to write down any instructions you have on how you want your spouse or family to post or update your social media accounts in your absence, whether you're away on vacation or business, sidelined by an illness or otherwise unable to handle things on your own – if you know what we mean. And yes, you'll find a document for that later on in the book.

My Social Life

My Social Life			
Facebook			
Facebook User Name One	**URL to use when logging in**	**Email Address for Account**	**Password**
What I use the account for	**Instructions/Notes**		
Facebook User Name Two	**URL to use when logging in**	**Email Address for Account**	**Password**
What I use the account for	**Instructions/Notes**		
Twitter			
Twitter User Name One	**URL to use when logging in**	**Email Address for Account**	**Password**
What I use the account for	**Instructions/Notes**		
Twitter User Name Two	**URL to use when logging in**	**Email Address for Account**	**Password**
What I use the account for	**Instructions/Notes**		

Google Plus			
Google Plus User Name	**URL to use when logging in**	**Email Address for Account**	**Password**
What I use the account for	**Instructions/Notes**		

Linked In			
Linked In User Name	**URL to use when logging in**	**Email Address for Account**	**Password**
What I use the account for	**Instructions/Notes**		

YouTube or Other Video Sharing Services			
User Name	**URL to use when logging in**	**Email Address for Account**	**Password**
What I use the account for	**Instructions/Notes**		
User Name	**URL to use when logging in**	**Email Address for Account**	**Password**
What I use the account for	**Instructions/Notes**		

	Pinterest		
Pinterest User Name	**URL to use when logging in**	**Email Address for Account**	**Password**
What I use the account for	**Instructions/Notes**		

	Flickr/Picassa or Other Photo Sharing Sites		
User Name One	**URL to use when logging in**	**Email Address for Account**	**Password**
What I use the account for	**Instructions/Notes**		
User Name Two	**URL to use when logging in**	**Email Address for Account**	**Password**
What I use the account for	**Instructions/Notes**		

	iTunes or Other Music Sharing Sites		
User Name One	**URL to use when logging in**	**Email Address for Account**	**Password**
What I use the account for	**Instructions/Notes**		
User Name Two	**URL to use when logging in**	**Email Address for Account**	**Password**
What I use the account for	**Instructions/Notes**		

	Blog		
Name of Blog	**URL to use when logging in**	**User ID**	**Password**
Email Account Associated	**Instructions/Notes**		

	Cloud or File Storage Sites		
User Name One	**URL to use when logging in**	**Email Address for Account**	**Password**
What I Store There	**Instructions/Notes**		
User Name Two	**URL to use when logging in**	**Email Address for Account**	**Password**
What I Store There	**Instructions/Notes**		

	Kindle, Nook or Other Book Download Sites		
User Name One	**URL to use when logging in**	**Email Address for Account**	**Password**
What I use the account for	**Instructions/Notes**		
User Name Two	**URL to use when logging in**	**Email Address for Account**	**Password**
What I use the account for	**Instructions/Notes**		

Voice Mail Accounts			
For Cell? Home? Work?	**Dial In Number**	**Password**	**Other Codes**
Instructions/Notes			
For Cell? Home? Work?	**Dial In Number**	**Password**	**Other Codes**
Instructions/Notes			
For Cell? Home? Work?	**Dial In Number**	**Password**	**Other Codes**
Instructions/Notes			

Other Social Media			
Website	**URL to use when logging in**	**Email Address for Account**	**Password**
What I use the account for	**Instructions/Notes**		

Other Social Media			
Website	**URL to use when logging in**	**Email Address for Account**	**Password**
What I use the account for	**Instructions/Notes**		

Other Social Media			
Website	**URL to use when logging in**	**Email Address for Account**	**Password**
What I use the account for	**Instructions/Notes**		

Other Social Media			
Website	**URL to use when logging in**	**Email Address for Account**	**Password**
What I use the account for	**Instructions/Notes**		

Section Two	My Personal Email Addresses		
Email Address One	**URL to use when logging in**	**User ID**	**Password**
What I use the account for	**Instructions/Notes**		
Email Address Two	**URL to use when logging in**	**User ID**	**Password**
What I use the account for	**Instructions/Notes**		
Email Address Three	**URL to use when logging in**	**User ID**	**Password**
What I use the account for	**Instructions/Notes**		

Email Address Four	URL to use when logging in	User ID	Password

What I use the account for	Instructions/Notes		

My Work Email

My Work Email Address 1	URL to use when logging in	User ID	Password

What I use the account for	Instructions/Notes		

My Work Email Address 2	URL to use when logging in	User ID	Password

What I use the account for	Instructions/Notes		

My Work Benefits

My User ID/Password	URL to use when logging in

Type of Benefits	Name and contact information for HR Representative

Customer Service	Instructions/Notes (include people who can help some access your benefits information for you, in your absence)

Section Three — Internet Memberships

In this section note any Internet memberships with recurring fees like Netflix, Hulu, news services or professional organizations.

Website	Type of Membership	URL to use when logging in	User ID

Password	Fee/Term	Member Number	

Website	Type of Membership	URL to use when logging in	User ID
Password	Fee/Term	Member Number	
Website	Type of Membership	URL to use when logging in	User ID
Password	Fee/Term	Member Number	
Website	Type of Membership	URL to use when logging in	User ID
Password	Fee/Term	Member Number	
Website	Type of Membership	URL to use when logging in	User ID
Password	Fee/Term	Member Number	
Website	Type of Membership	URL to use when logging in	User ID
Password	Fee/Term	Member Number	

Section Four	Other Websites I Frequently Use	
Website		URL to use when logging in
User ID		Password
Website		URL to use when logging in
User ID		Password
Website		URL to use when logging in
User ID		Password

Website	URL to use when logging in
User ID	Password
Website	URL to use when logging in
User ID	Password

My Business Life Forms

Your Business Life Forms

If you're an entrepreneur, you already know what it takes to run a successful business.

You think nothing of having to wear twenty or thirty hats at once and the amount of information you have to keep in your head, especially if your business is internet-based, is astounding.

But what happens if you want to enjoy your success. Let's say you want to just take off and go to Maui for two weeks. Or what if you can't run your business for a few weeks due to injury or illness?

If all of that information that you use to run your business on a daily business is in your head, or worse, scrawled on little post it notes stuck all over your desk and floor, how is anyone going to step in and run things for you while you're gone? Do you have all of that information in a place where your partner or colleague can step in and seamlessly take over?

Now you do! Because that is what the book is all about. You now have a place – physically and virtually – to record all of the information that it takes to keep your business running. Just in case you finally decide to take that vacation!

If you've already downloaded the forms that come with this book, you have everything you need to keep all of the information it takes to run your business, at your fingertips. The best part is, if your business partner or someone acting in your behalf ever needs that information ASAP, you or they can simply retrieve it. Which means that you'll now be able to deal with emergencies large or small, even if you're off vacationing in Maui.

Once you've completed the Business Life forms we suggest that you save and store them in at least three secure locations, preferably away from home – just in case. Besides the copy that you'll save to your iCloud or Microsoft SkyDrive account, save your files **on a password-protected flash drive or portable hard drive:**

- And place it in a safe deposit box or water/fireproof safe in your own city.
- And place it in a safe deposit box, water/fireproof safe, or with relatives in the city where you'll be evacuating.
- Or place the forms and documents in a password-protected online file repository or the file directory of your web site.
- And take it with you on a key ring or in an emergency evacuation bin, if you ever have to evacuate your building or home office.

You can also simply fill in the forms right in the book and toss it into waterproof/fireproof safe, locking file cabinet, safe deposit box, or your lawyer's office. It's up to you.

So if you haven't already done it, take a moment to download the free digital versions of each form using the link that you'll find at the beginning of the book.

My Business Life

My Business Email Addresses

Email Address One	What URL to use when logging in	User ID	Password
What I use the account for	Instructions/Notes		
Email Address Two	What URL to use when logging in	User ID	Password
What I use the account for	Instructions/Notes		
Email Address Three	What URL to use when logging in	User ID	Password
What I use the account for	Instructions/Notes		
Email Address Four	What URL to use when logging in	User ID	Password
What I use the account for	Instructions/Notes		
Email Address Five	What URL to use when logging in	User ID	Password
What I use the account for	Instructions/Notes		
Email Address Six	What URL to use when logging in	User ID	Password
What I use the account for	Instructions/Notes		

Section Two	**Business Websites**		
Website One	Web Hosting Service	URL to use for Login	User ID
Password	Term of Service	Payment Amount/When Due	How To Pay
Customer Service	Who else can access or update this website?	What I use this account for	
Instructions/Notes			
Website Two	Web Hosting Service	URL to use for Login	User ID
Password	Term of Service	Payment Amount/When Due	How To Pay
Customer Service	Who else can access or update this website?	What I use this account for	
Instructions/Notes			
Website Three	Web Hosting Service	URL to use for Login	User ID
Password	Term of Service	Payment Amount/When Due	How To Pay
Customer Service	Who else can access or update this website?	What I use this account for	
Instructions/Notes			

Section Three	Pay Pal or Shopping Cart Management Accounts		
I manage my customer shopping cart through:	URL to use for Login	User ID	Password
Term of Service	Payment Amount/When Due	How To Pay for Service	Customer Service
When sales come in, what account do they go into?	Account Number	Password and instructions for managing or withdrawing money from that	
Who else can access or update this shopping cart?	How often are sales transferred into my	Instructions/Notes For Shopping Cart	
I manage my alternate customer shopping cart through:	URL to use for Login	User ID	Password
Term of Service	Payment Amount/When Due	How To Pay for Service	Customer Service
When sales come in, what account do they go into?	Account Number	Password and instructions for managing or withdrawing money from that	
Who else can access or update this shopping cart?	How often are sales transferred into my	Instructions/Notes For Shopping Cart	
Instructions/Notes			

Section Four	Contractors/Virtual Assistants		
I hire and use workers through this company	URL to use for Login	User ID	Password
Term of Service	How To Pay for Service	Customer Service	Others who have
Workers I currently or have employed		Contact information and notes	
Alternate Company	URL to use for Login	User ID	Password
Term of Service	How To Pay for Service	Customer Service	Others who have
Workers I currently or have employed		Instructions and Notes	

Section Five	Affiliate Accounts (like Amazon or Click Bank)		
Affiliate Account 1	URL to use for Login	User ID	Password
When sales/money come in, what account do they go into?	Account Number	Password and instructions for managing or withdrawing money from that account.	
Who else can update this affiliate account?	How often are sales transferred into my	Instructions/Notes For affiliate account	
Affiliate Account 2	URL to use for Login	User ID	Password
When sales/money come in, what account do they go into?	Account Number	Password and instructions for managing or withdrawing money from that account.	
Who else can update this affiliate account?	How often are sales transferred into my	Instructions/Notes For affiliate account	
Affiliate Account 3	URL to use for Login	User ID	Password
When sales/money come in, what account do they go into?	Account Number	Password and instructions for managing or withdrawing money from that account.	
Who else can update this affiliate account?	How often are sales transferred into my	Instructions/Notes For affiliate account	

Section Six	Publishing Accounts (like Create Space, or Lulu		
Publishing Account 1	URL to use for Login	User ID	Password
Which books are published through this	URL to use for editing books	Titles/ISBNs	
When sales/money come in, what account do they go into?	Account Number	Password and instructions for managing or withdrawing money from that account.	
Who else can update this publishing account?	How often are sales transferred into my	Instructions/Notes For publishing account	
Publishing Account 2	URL to use for Login	User ID	Password
Which books are published through this	URL to use for editing books	Titles/ISBNs	
When sales/money come in, what account do they go into?	Account Number	Password and instructions for managing or withdrawing money from that account.	
Who else can update this publishing account?	How often are sales transferred into my	Instructions/Notes For publishing account	
Publishing Account 3	URL to use for Login	User ID	Password
Which books are published through this	URL to use for editing books	Titles/ISBNs	
When sales/money come in, what account do they go into?	Account Number	Password and instructions for managing or withdrawing money from that account.	
Who else can update this publishing account?	How often are sales transferred into my	Instructions/Notes For publishing account	

Section Seven	Email List Management Accounts (like Constant Contact or A Weber)		
I manage my customer email list through:	URL to use for Login	User ID	Password
Term of Service	Payment Amount/When Due	How To Pay for Service	Customer Service
Who else can access or update this account?	How often do I sent out email updates?	Instructions/Notes For Email Management Account	
My alternate customer email list is through:	URL to use for Login	User ID	Password
Term of Service	Payment Amount/When Due	How To Pay for Service	Customer Service
Who else can access or update this account?	How often do I sent out email updates?	Instructions/Notes For Email Management Account	

Section Eight	Business Bank Accounts		
Bank	Account Number	Branch	Checking /Savings?
Website	User Name/PIN	Customer Service	Notes
Bank	Account Number	Branch	Checking /Savings?
Website	User Name/PIN	Customer Service	Notes

Section Nine	**Our Business Structure**		
Legal Name of Company 1	Tax ID#	Type of Company (partnership/LLC/Sole Prop)	

Business Address	Principals	Board Members	Investors

Where I keep the business articles of incorporation and corporate documents		Who else has access to this information or can help in your absence? Name,	

Legal Name of Company 2	Tax ID#	Type of Company (partnership/LLC/Sole Prop)	

Business Address	Principals	Board Members	Investors

Where I keep the business articles of incorporation and corporate documents		Who else has access to this information or can help in your absence? Name,	

Section Ten			Business Credit Cards			
Card 1/Type			Account Number		Website	User Name/PIN
Credit Limit	Interest Rate			Customer Service		Notes
Card 2/Type		Account Number		Website		User Name/PIN
Credit Limit	Interest Rate		Customer Service		Notes	
Card 3/Type		Account Number		Website		User Name/PIN
Credit Limit	Interest Rate		Customer Service		Notes	

Section Eleven	Office Rental Information		
Management Company	Rent	Date Due	End Date of Lease
Management Phone	Payment Address		

Section Twelve		Business Insurance	
Insurance Company	Member Number	Group/Policy Number	Customer Service
Type	Agent Name	Agent Number	Notes
Insurance Company	Member Number	Group/Policy Number	Customer Service
Type	Agent Name	Agent Number	Notes

Section Thirteen		Memberships/ID Cards	

In this section note any memberships you pay for, ie. the gym, professional organizations, book clubs, or other recurring payments

Gym Membership	Location	Member Number	Renewal Date
Other Membership	Location	Member Number	Renewal Date
Other Membership	Type	Member Number	Renewal Date
Other Membership	Type	Member Number	Renewal Date
Other Membership	Type	Member Number	Renewal Date
Other Membership	Type	Member Number	Renewal Date

Section Fourteen	My Business' Social Life		
	Facebook		

Facebook User Name One	URL to use when logging in	Email Address for Account	Password

What I use the account for	Instructions/Notes		

Facebook User Name Two	URL to use when logging in	Email Address for Account	Password

What I use the account for	Instructions/Notes		

	Twitter		

Twitter User Name One	URL to use when logging in	Email Address for Account	Password

What I use the account for	Instructions/Notes		

Twitter User Name Two	URL to use when logging in	Email Address for Account	Password

What I use the account for	Instructions/Notes		

Google Plus			
Google Plus User Name	**URL to use when logging in**	**Email Address for Account**	**Password**
What I use the account for	**Instructions/Notes**		

Linked In			
Linked In User Name	**URL to use when logging in**	**Email Address for Account**	**Password**
What I use the account for	**Instructions/Notes**		

YouTube or Other Video Sharing Services			
User Name	**URL to use when logging in**	**Email Address for Account**	**Password**
What I use the account for	**Instructions/Notes**		
User Name	**URL to use when logging in**	**Email Address for Account**	**Password**
What I use the account for	**Instructions/Notes**		

	Pinterest		
Pinterest User Name	**URL to use when logging in**	**Email Address for Account**	**Password**
What I use the account for	**Instructions/Notes**		

	Flickr/Picassa/Instagram or Other Photo Sharing Sites		
User Name One	**URL to use when logging in**	**Email Address for Account**	**Password**
What I use the account for	**Instructions/Notes**		
User Name Two	**URL to use when logging in**	**Email Address for Account**	**Password**
What I use the account for	**Instructions/Notes**		

	iTunes or Other Music Sharing Sites		
User Name One	**URL to use when logging in**	**Email Address for Account**	**Password**
What I use the account for	**Instructions/Notes**		

User Name Two	URL to use when logging in	Email Address for Account	Password

What I use the account for	Instructions/Notes		

Blog

Name of Blog	URL to use when logging in	User ID	Password

Email Account Associated	Instructions/Notes		

Name of Blog	URL to use when logging in	User ID	Password

Email Account Associated	Instructions/Notes		

Cloud or File Storage Sites

User Name One	URL to use when logging in	Email Address for Account	Password

What I Store There	Instructions/Notes		

User Name Two	URL to use when logging in	Email Address for Account	Password

What I Store There	Instructions/Notes		

Kindle, Nook or Other Book Download Sites

User Name One	URL to use when logging in	Email Address for Account	Password

What I use the account for	Instructions/Notes

User Name Two	URL to use when logging in	Email Address for Account	Password

What I use the account for	Instructions/Notes

Voice Mail Accounts

For Cell? Home? Work?	Dial In Number	Password	Other Codes

Instructions/Notes

For Cell? Home? Work?	Dial In Number	Password	Other Codes

Instructions/Notes

For Cell? Home? Work?	Dial In Number	Password	Other Codes

Instructions/Notes

Other Social Media			
Website	URL to use when logging in	Email Address for Account	Password
What I use the account for	Instructions/Notes		

Other Social Media			
Website	URL to use when logging in	Email Address for Account	Password
What I use the account for	Instructions/Notes		

Other Social Media			
Website	URL to use when logging in	Email Address for Account	Password
What I use the account for	Instructions/Notes		

Other Social Media			
Website	URL to use when logging in	Email Address for Account	Password
What I use the account for	Instructions/Notes		

Other Social Media			
Website	**URL to use when logging in**	**Email Address for Account**	**Password**
What I use the account for	**Instructions/Notes**		

Other Social Media			
Website	**URL to use when logging in**	**Email Address for Account**	**Password**
What I use the account for	**Instructions/Notes**		

Section Fifteen		Internet Memberships	
In this section note any website memberships you pay for, ie. professional organizations, training programs, Netflix, or other recurring payments			
Membership	Type	Member Number	Renewal Date
Other Membership	Type	Member Number	Renewal Date
Other Membership	Type	Member Number	Renewal Date
Other Membership	Type	Member Number	Renewal Date
Other Membership	Type	Member Number	Renewal Date
Other Membership	Type	Member Number	Renewal Date
Other Membership	Type	Member Number	Renewal Date
Other Membership	Type	Member Number	Renewal Date
Other Membership	Type	Member Number	Renewal Date
Other Membership	Type	Member Number	Renewal Date
Other Membership	Type	Member Number	Renewal Date
Other Membership	Type	Member Number	Renewal Date

Other Membership	Type	Member Number	Renewal Date
Other Membership	Type	Member Number	Renewal Date
Other Membership	Type	Member Number	Renewal Date
Other Membership	Type	Member Number	Renewal Date
Other Membership	Type	Member Number	Renewal Date
Other Membership	Type	Member Number	Renewal Date

Section Sixteen		Other Websites That I Often Use		
Website Name	Log In URL	User Name	Password	What I use it for
Website Name	Log In URL	User Name	Password	What I use it for
Website Name	Log In URL	User Name	Password	What I use it for
Website Name	Log In URL	User Name	Password	What I use it for
Website Name	Log In URL	User Name	Password	What I use it for
Website Name	Log In URL	User Name	Password	What I use it for
Website Name	Log In URL	User Name	Password	What I use it for
Website Name	Log In URL	User Name	Password	What I use it for
Website Name	Log In URL	User Name	Password	What I use it for
Website Name	Log In URL	User Name	Password	What I use it for
Website Name	Log In URL	User Name	Password	What I use it for
Website Name	Log In URL	User Name	Password	What I use it for
Website Name	Log In URL	User Name	Password	What I use it for

Website Name	Log In URL	User Name	Password	What I use it for
Website Name	Log In URL	User Name	Password	What I use it for
Website Name	Log In URL	User Name	Password	What I use it for
Website Name	Log In URL	User Name	Password	What I use it for
Website Name	Log In URL	User Name	Password	What I use it for

Office Inventory

The Office Inventory was created to give you a place to record all of your computers, monitors, office machines, and valuable electronics, along with the model and serial numbers, warranty and the location of any additional information. Before you begin, tour your office room by room, noting any of those items. Take a photograph of the current condition of each item before you enter it below, or videotape your office, showing each item in detail. If those items are ever lost or damaged, it would help you file an insurance claim. Store the photos/video with this inventory. Don't forget that you'll find a copy of this form in the downloadable files that came with the book. Just complete them on your computer or print out as many as you need.

Item	Manufacturer	Model	Serial Number
Warranty Number	Expiration Number	Location of Photo/Link to Video Tour/Notes	
Item	Manufacturer	Model	Serial Number
Warranty Number	Expiration Number	Location of Photo/Link to Video Tour/Notes	
Item	Manufacturer	Model	Serial Number
Warranty Number	Expiration Number	Location of Photo/Link to Video Tour/Notes	
Item	Manufacturer	Model	Serial Number
Warranty Number	Expiration Number	Location of Photo/Link to Video Tour/Notes	
Item	Manufacturer	Model	Serial Number
Warranty Number	Expiration Number	Location of Photo/Link to Video Tour/Notes	
Item	Manufacturer	Model	Serial Number
Warranty Number	Expiration Number	Location of Photo/Link to Video Tour/Notes	
Item	Manufacturer	Model	Serial Number
Warranty Number	Expiration Number	Location of Photo/Link to Video Tour/Notes	

Item	Manufacturer	Model	Serial Number

Warranty Number	Expiration Number	Location of Photo/Link to Video Tour/Notes	

Item	Manufacturer	Model	Serial Number

Warranty Number	Expiration Number	Location of Photo/Link to Video Tour/Notes	

Item	Manufacturer	Model	Serial Number

Warranty Number	Expiration Number	Location of Photo/Link to Video Tour/Notes	

Item	Manufacturer	Model	Serial Number

Warranty Number	Expiration Number	Location of Photo/Link to Video Tour/Notes	

Item	Manufacturer	Model	Serial Number

Warranty Number	Expiration Number	Location of Photo/Link to Video Tour/Notes	

Item	Manufacturer	Model	Serial Number

Warranty Number	Expiration Number	Location of Photo/Link to Video Tour/Notes	

Item	Manufacturer	Model	Serial Number

Warranty Number	Expiration Number	Location of Photo/Link to Video Tour/Notes	

Item	Manufacturer	Model	Serial Number

Warranty Number	Expiration Number	Location of Photo/Link to Video Tour/Notes	

Item	Manufacturer	Model	Serial Number

Warranty Number	Expiration Number	Location of Photo/Link to Video Tour/Notes	

My Social Media Will

Deciding How You Want Your Social Media to be Handled

As much as you like to think that you'll always be able to manage your own email and social media accounts, every now and then things happen that make that difficult if not impossible. Since your email, Facebook, Twitter and other accounts are an important part of your life, it only makes sense to have a say in how things are managed in your absence. That's what this section is all about. Use the paragraphs below to communicate your wishes if you are unable to manage your social media accounts due to illness, extended absence or death.

You can complete this section any way that you'd like. If you need more space, use the digital version where you can add more social media accounts or make each section as long as you like to give yourself additional room. You can also:

- Have a separate section for your wishes if you become ill and can't maintain your accounts for a few weeks (like being holed up in Gstaad with a broken leg while skiing). This could include who will keep things going for you and how you want things maintained until you're back in charge.
- Have a section on how you want your accounts continued, memorialized or deleted after your death.
- Have a section with instructions on how to save or delete any materials on those sites, like photos and videos. Are there any people who should receive those photos or videos, or do you want them copied and shared among several people?
- Do you want any final messages or posts uploaded to any specific accounts?
- And anything else you wish to communicate....

Believe it or not, even the government is now recommending that every adult should have a social media will. It not only enables them to specify all of their wishes, but gives their loved ones the passwords and user IDs they would need to access to their social media accounts, if they are incapacitated.

This document can be printed and saved as a part of your will or you can save it separately and simply provide your loved ones with a link to it or include the location of the form in your will. It's up to you. Since wills are technically public documents, you might not want to include this form in your actual will. Just make sure that the person who will be acting as your executor/executrix and your attorney know where to locate this form if it is ever needed. And make sure that you update it every few months, to include any new accounts or changes to current accounts and passwords.

Finally, store this form in at least three safe places.
- Store it on a password protected file on your computer hard drive.
- Store it on a password protected flash or portable hard drive and place it in your local safe deposit box.
- Store it on a password protected flash or portable hard drive and place it in your a safe deposit box in your pre-determined evacuation location.

If you feel safe doing so, you can also store it along with your will at your attorney's office.

My Social Media Will

Here Are My Wishes for Maintaining My Facebook Account If I Become Incapacitated

Here Are My Wishes for Maintaining My Facebook Account After My Death

Here Are My Wishes for Maintaining My Twitter Account If I Become Incapacitated

Here Are My Wishes for Maintaining My Twitter Account After My Death

Here Are My Wishes for Maintaining My YouTube or Video Accounts If I Become Incapacitated

Here Are My Wishes for Maintaining My YouTube or Video Accounts After My Death

Here Are My Wishes for Maintaining My Blog If I Become Incapacitated

Here Are My Wishes for Maintaining My Blog After My Death

Here Are My Wishes for Maintaining My Online File Storage If I Become Incapacitated

Here Are My Wishes for Maintaining My Online File Storage After My Death

Here Are My Wishes for Maintaining My _____ Account If I Become Incapacitated

Here Are My Wishes for Maintaining My _____ Account After My Death

Here Are My Wishes for Maintaining My _____ Account If I Become Incapacitated

Here Are My Wishes for Maintaining My _____ Account After My Death

Here Are My Wishes for Maintaining My _____ Account If I Become Incapacitated

Here Are My Wishes for Maintaining My _____ Account After My Death

Here Are My Wishes for Maintaining My _____ Account If I Become Incapacitated

Here Are My Wishes for Maintaining My _____ Account After My Death

Here Are My Wishes for Maintaining My _____ Account If I Become Incapacitated

Here Are My Wishes for Maintaining My _____ Account After My Death

Here Are My Wishes for Maintaining My _____ Account If I Become Incapacitated

Here Are My Wishes for Maintaining My _____ Account After My Death

Here Are My Wishes for Maintaining My _____ Account If I Become Incapacitated

Here Are My Wishes for Maintaining My _____ Account After My Death

Here Are My Wishes for Maintaining My _____ Account If I Become Incapacitated

Here Are My Wishes for Maintaining My _____ Account After My Death

Here Are My Wishes for Maintaining My _____ Account If I Become Incapacitated

Here Are My Wishes for Maintaining My _____ Account After My Death

Here Are My Wishes for Maintaining My _____ Account If I Become Incapacitated

Here Are My Wishes for Maintaining My _____ Account After My Death

Here Are My Wishes for Maintaining My _____ Account If I Become Incapacitated

Here Are My Wishes for Maintaining My _____ Account After My Death

Here Are My Wishes for Maintaining My _____ Account If I Become Incapacitated

Here Are My Wishes for Maintaining My _____ Account After My Death

 **MEET THE WHOLE FAMILY**

Available at **amazon** &  gumroad

You can find all of our books – both paperback and instant PDF downloads – on the Books tab of our website www.getyourstufftogether.com.

Get Our Books At Bulk Rates For Your Business, Church, Service Club or Organization! Email Us Through The Website For Details.

 **GET YOUR STUFF TOGETHER**

 **MEET THE WHOLE FAMILY**

Available at
 B O N F I R E

A percentage of each product sold will go towards putting our newest book *#Alone Together*, into the hands of the families who need it. The book's mission? To help keep hospitalized COVID-19 patients from dying alone, by giving their families the tools they need to stay connected with them and their medical team.

To purchase masks, mugs & tee shirts   https://www.bonfire.com/store/getyourstufftogether/
To purchase phone cases   https://www.zazzle.com/s/wealthoftulips+phone+cases

Richly Red Smile Mask

Creativi-Tea Coffee &Tea Mug

Prosperi-Tee Tee Shirt

Pretty In Pink Smile Mask

Leftea Coffee &Tea Mug

Creativi-Tee Tee Shirt

Red Parrot Tulip Phone Case

Personali-Tee Tee Shirt

Tulips In Breeze Phone Case

GET YOUR STUFF TOGETHER MERCHANDISE

About The Authors

Janet and Laura are one of the only mother/daughter writing teams in the entertainment industry. They began their careers in production on network sitcoms at MGM and Warner Bros and are currently developing their own original movies and television series.

The Greenwalds were introduced to emergency preparedness the hard way, when a jumbo-jet crashed across the street from their home. But it was a horrendous medical tragedy – one that took the life of their mother/grandmother, Elaine Sullivan – that propelled them into new territory.

When Elaine's hospital failed to notify Jan and Laura of her hospitalization they were not only prevented from being at her side, but they were also kept from preventing the drug interaction that took Elaine's life.

After uncovering a loophole in the laws which regulate the notification of the next of kin of hospital patients, Laura & Jan joined forces with legislators in Illinois and California to enact three Next of Kin Laws, before creating Notify In 7, a training program that provides hospital professionals with the skills they need to notify and reunite trauma victims with their loved ones, quickly and easily. Hoping to keep other families from experiencing the same thing they had, they turned their story into a screenplay called Without Consent, now in development as a feature film.

Their book *Keep Everything You Love Safe*, gives readers quick and easy steps they can take to keep everything that's important to them organized, safe and accessible. Each section – over 30 in all – covers a different area from backing up & fixing family photos, home movies and music, to creating an evacuation plan, securing vital documents, medical information, financial information and data.

Between their books, blog and website, over 1.5 million people have used Jan and Laura's shortcut sheets, action plans and materials to keep themselves, their homes, their families and the things that they love, safe and secure.

www.ingramcontent.com/pod-product-compliance
Lightning Source LLC
Chambersburg PA
CBHW082111070326
40689CB00052B/4606